Hard Riddles

For Teens, Adults and Genius Kids - #Stumped Volume 6

#STUMPED

Hard Riddles

"Are you a riddle genius?"

For Teens, Adults and Genius Kids
Stumped Volume 6

#StumpedRiddles are ideal for family gatherings, dinner parties, office parties, grad parties, and birthday parties. Basically, any place you're gathered together and in need of a game that lets you write or shout the answers out.

Or just have a party of one and try to solve them!

Also great for Gifts, Contests, Prizes, and Stocking Stuffers.

Self Published

Author: Barbara Tremblay Cipak

Copyright

Self Published by Barbara Tremblay Cipak, Toronto, Ontario, Canada

Copyright © 2020. All rights reserved.

No part of this book may be used or reproduced in any manner whatsoever without written permission except in the case of very brief quotations embodied in articles or reviews. If a riddle is used in part or in full, a link to this book and the author's name (Barbara Tremblay Cipak) must be provided alongside the riddle. No more than one riddle may be used in one review at a time. And thank you.

Barbara (Tremblay) Cipak has personally written all riddles in this book. Any resemblance to people, characters, businesses, organizations, places, events, other riddles, and incidents either are the product of the author's imagination/experiences or are fictitious. Any resemblance to actual persons, living or dead, events, or locales is entirely coincidental, unless otherwise clearly stated by the author. But let's face it, riddles don't resemble people's lives, or do they?

For information contact: admin@stumpedriddles.com, Barbara Cipak, Toronto, Ontario Canada

ISBN: 9798557171670
Hard Riddles: For Teens, Adults and Genius Kids - Stumped Volume 6

Dedicated
To
Those Who Love
to Challenge
Their Mind

Riddle Games

Party Games

Riddle games are ideal for parties, family gatherings, birthday parties, grad parties, or for a party of one. The best and worst riddle guessers get a prize or bragging rights, you choose.

Game 1

- Use a Timer
- Decide upon the amount of time to allow
- Read the Riddle
- Everyone shouts out answers
- The first one to guess the answer gets a point

Game 2

- Read the Riddle (with or without a timer)
- Everyone writes down their answer
- Put the answers in the middle
- Each person who guesses correctly gets a point

If nobody correctly guesses a riddle, everyone subtracts a point and goes backward on their total.

NOTE:
The background photo featured on some of the riddles are subtle, indirect clues to the riddle answer.

Table of Contents

Copyright..3

Dedicated...4

Riddle Games..5

Chapter One Human Qualities...7

Chapter Two Human Emotions & Feelings.................................19

Chapter Three Homonyms..30

Chapter Four are Homograph Words...41

Chapter Five Triple Homophones..52

Chapter Six Double Homophones...63

Chapter Seven Words With "Q" in Them...................................74

Chapter Eight are Four Syllable Words......................................85

Answer Section..96

    Chapter One Answers..97

    Chapter Two Answers..98

    Chapter Three Answers...99

    Chapter Four Answers...100

    Chapter Five Answers..101

    Chapter Six Answers...102

    Chapter Seven Answers..103

Chapter Eight Answers..104

Back Cover Answer...105

About the Author..106

Why a Riddle Book?..107

Additional Riddle Books..108

Social Media Follows:...109

Write Your Own Riddle...110

Chapter One Human Qualities

"Here you'll find riddle answers that relate to human traits or characteristics"

Human Qualities And Traits

Riddle 1

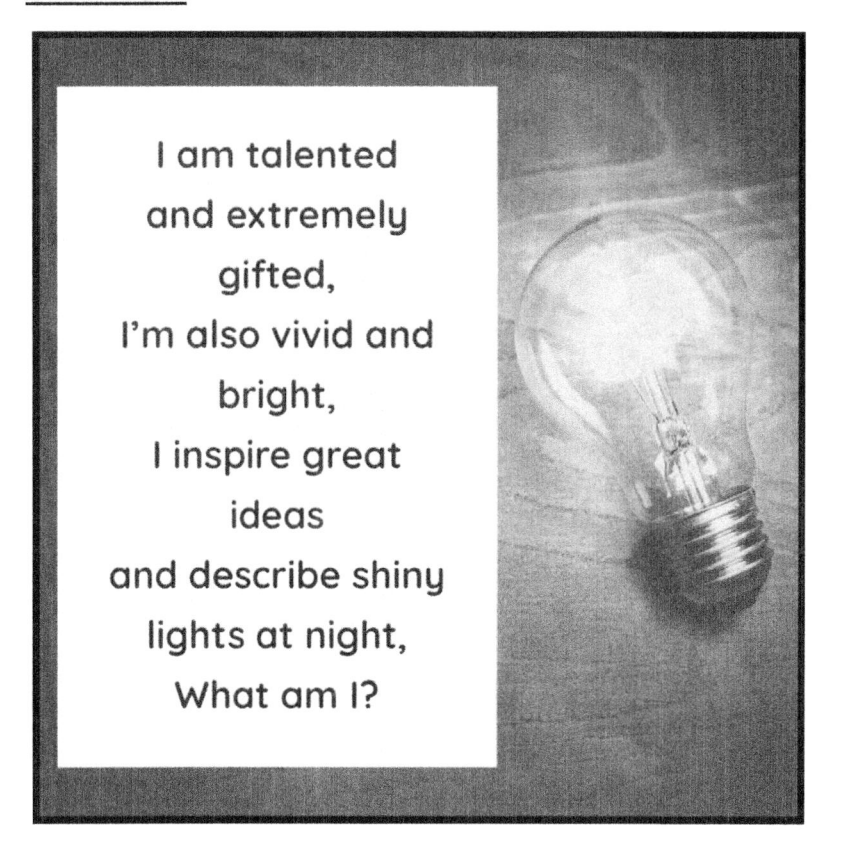

I am talented and extremely gifted,
I'm also vivid and bright,
I inspire great ideas
and describe shiny lights at night,
What am I?

Riddle 2

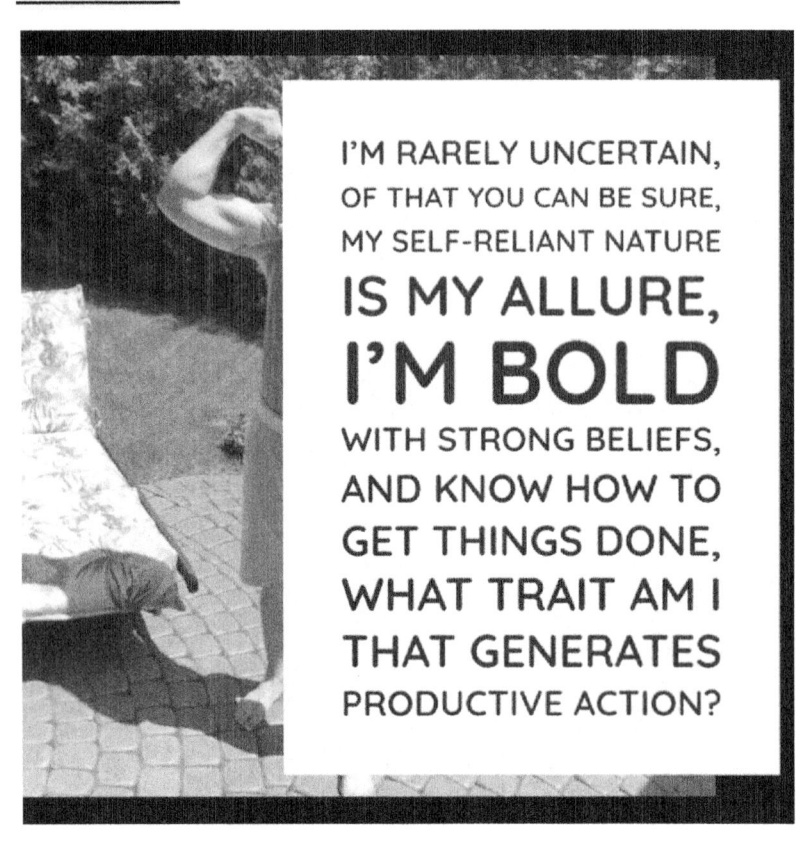

I'M RARELY UNCERTAIN,
OF THAT YOU CAN BE SURE,
MY SELF-RELIANT NATURE
**IS MY ALLURE,
I'M BOLD**
WITH STRONG BELIEFS,
AND KNOW HOW TO
GET THINGS DONE,
WHAT TRAIT AM I
THAT GENERATES
PRODUCTIVE ACTION?

Riddle 3

When you are this
with amounts,
toys,
time,
money,
and gifts,
you serve others
and your spirit
gets a lift,
What are you?

Riddle 4

I AM A WORD THAT'S NOT ALL THERE, FOR SOME IT'S HELL, A LIVING NIGHTMARE, THE MILDER ME IS USED TO ACCUSE PEOPLE OF CRAZY DEEDS, EVEN A GENIUS CAN BECOME ME, WHAT AM I?

Riddle 5

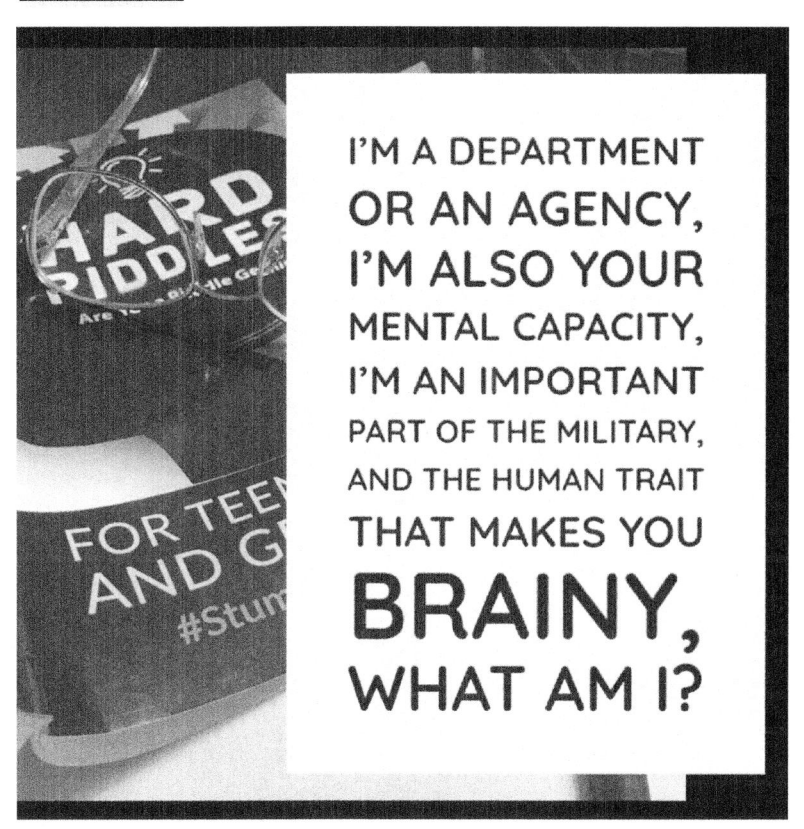

I'M A DEPARTMENT OR AN AGENCY, I'M ALSO YOUR MENTAL CAPACITY, I'M AN IMPORTANT PART OF THE MILITARY, AND THE HUMAN TRAIT THAT MAKES YOU **BRAINY**, WHAT AM I?

Riddle 6

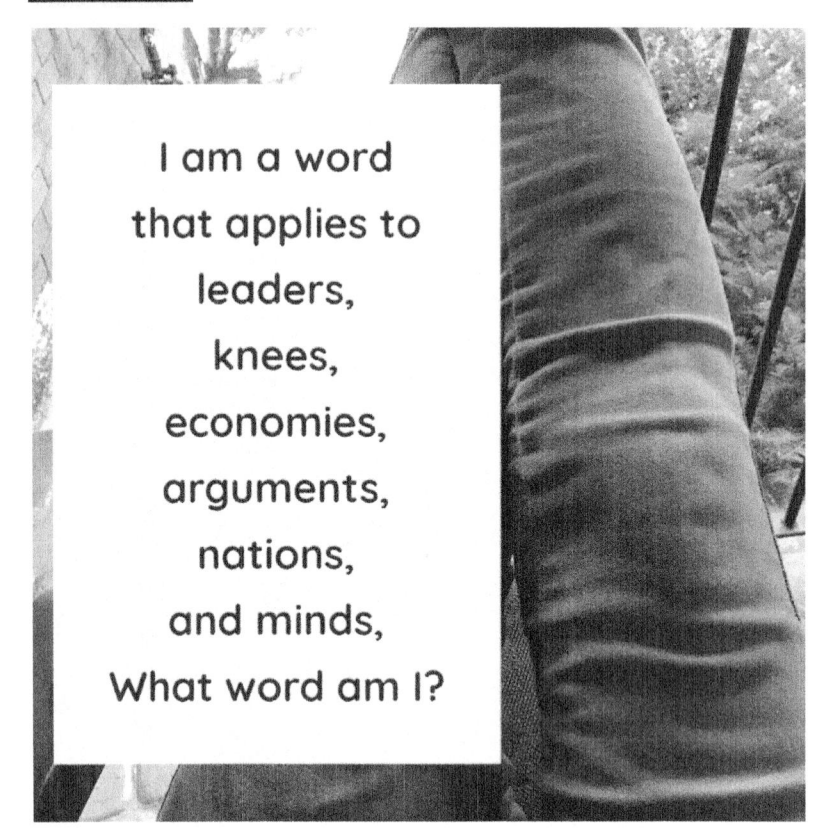

I am a word
that applies to
leaders,
knees,
economies,
arguments,
nations,
and minds,
What word am I?

Riddle 7

> I describe the water,
> wind, and your manner,
> and am the preferred
> state by most people,
> With me you'll feel
> centered and still,
> However, some can
> only achieve my tranquility
> by taking a prescription pill?
> What am I?

Riddle 8

This seven letter word
is part of a famous
George's name,
the needing-to-know
might drive you insane,
at least when you're this,
life isn't mundane,
What trait am I
that can keep your
brain in the game?

Riddle 9

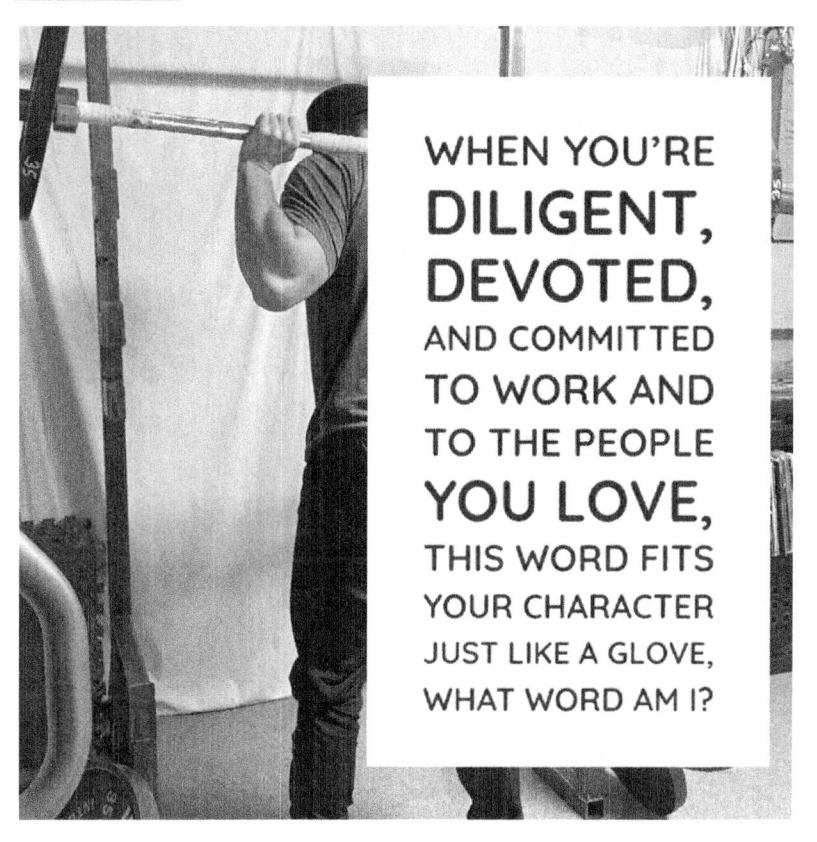

WHEN YOU'RE **DILIGENT, DEVOTED,** AND COMMITTED TO WORK AND TO THE PEOPLE **YOU LOVE,** THIS WORD FITS YOUR CHARACTER JUST LIKE A GLOVE, WHAT WORD AM I?

Riddle 10

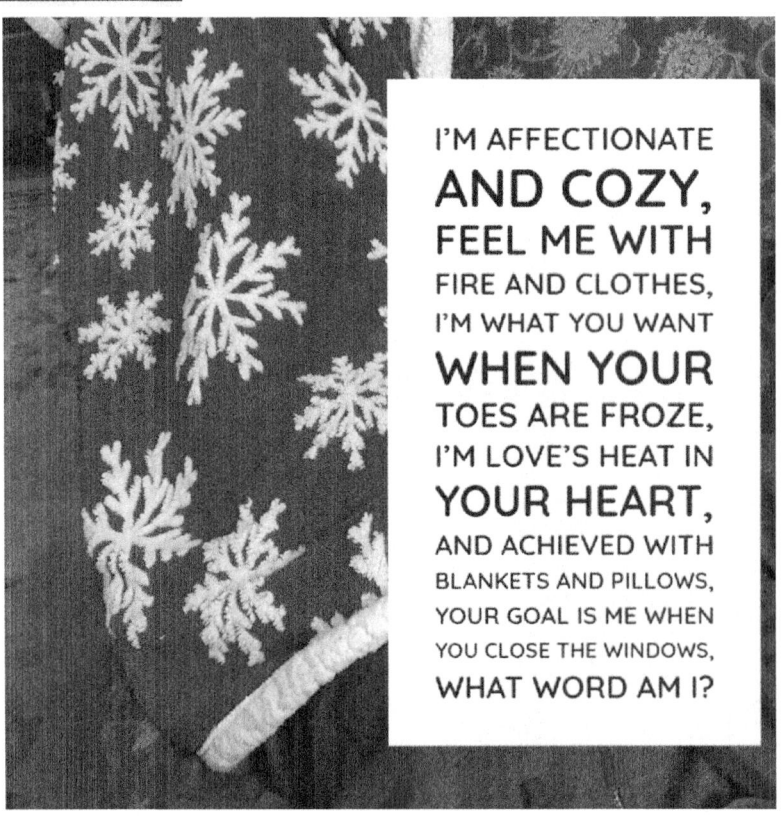

I'M AFFECTIONATE **AND COZY,** FEEL ME WITH FIRE AND CLOTHES, I'M WHAT YOU WANT **WHEN YOUR** TOES ARE FROZE, I'M LOVE'S HEAT IN **YOUR HEART,** AND ACHIEVED WITH BLANKETS AND PILLOWS, YOUR GOAL IS ME WHEN YOU CLOSE THE WINDOWS, **WHAT WORD AM I?**

Chapter Two Human Emotions & Feelings

"These riddle answers relate to life's emotions and feelings"

Emotions and Feelings

Riddle 11

> Whether influential
> or incredibly windy,
> this eight-letter word
> denotes both negative
> or positive authority,
> No matter which end
> of the spectrum
> strength is its trait; it's
> also physical or mental
> and doesn't apply
> to lightweights,
> What word is it?

Riddle 12

I can be both
your joy and
your dignity
or cause you to
behave boastfully,
When hunting in
a group, these animals
are also called me,
Some say I'm egotistical
but I can help you
approach life confidently,
What word am I?

Riddle 13

> This form of
> mental suffering
> is something
> nobody wants
> to go through,
> but the sad part is
> we all experience it
> when we bid
> those we love adieu,
> What is it?

Riddle 14

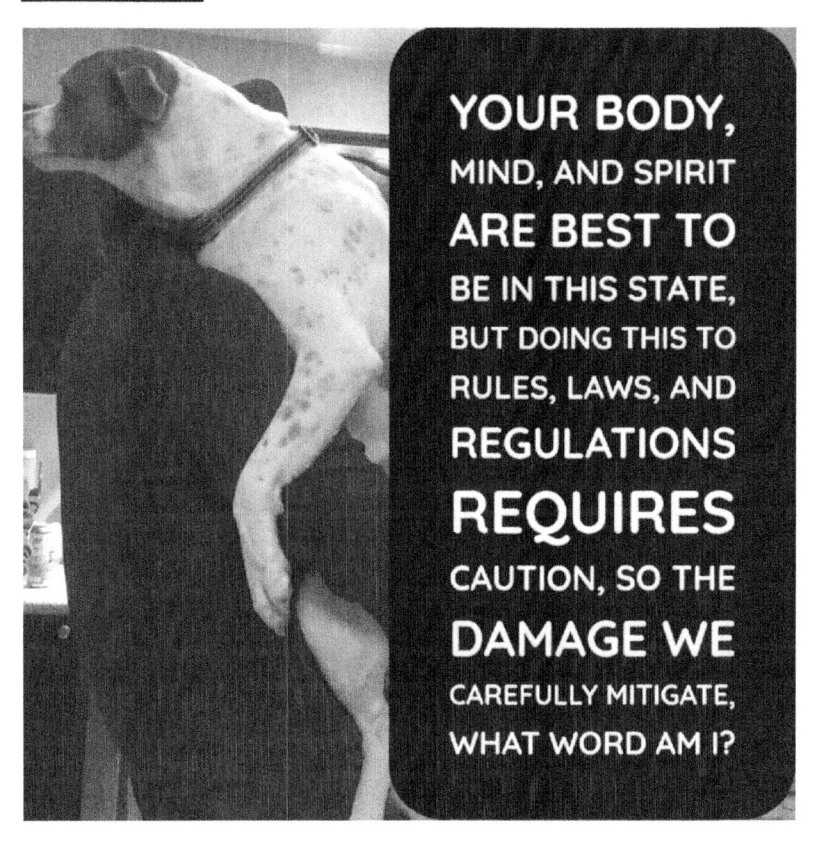

YOUR BODY, MIND, AND SPIRIT ARE BEST TO BE IN THIS STATE, BUT DOING THIS TO RULES, LAWS, AND REGULATIONS REQUIRES CAUTION, SO THE DAMAGE WE CAREFULLY MITIGATE, WHAT WORD AM I?

Riddle 15

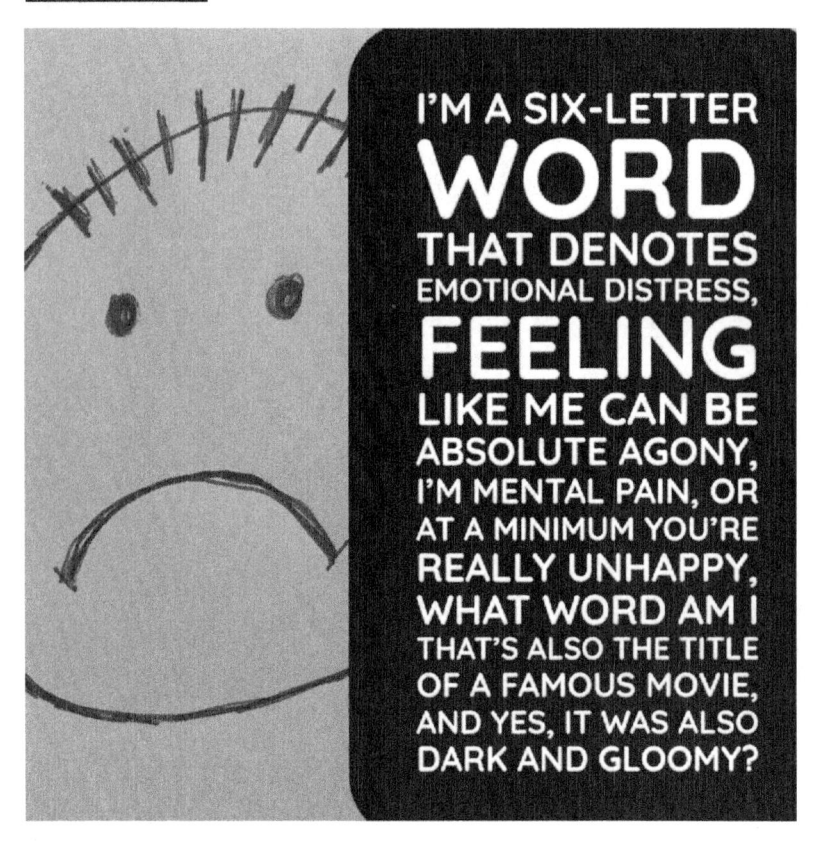

I'M A SIX-LETTER **WORD** THAT DENOTES EMOTIONAL DISTRESS, **FEELING** LIKE ME CAN BE ABSOLUTE AGONY, I'M MENTAL PAIN, OR AT A MINIMUM YOU'RE REALLY UNHAPPY, WHAT WORD AM I THAT'S ALSO THE TITLE OF A FAMOUS MOVIE, AND YES, IT WAS ALSO DARK AND GLOOMY?

Riddle 16

I'm mental,
physical,
minor,
major,
phantom
and killer,
What word am I
that nobody
wants or likes,
and can even be
caused by something small,
like a sliver?

Riddle 17

> You're in a fog
> and rather dazed,
> let's hope this feeling
> is just a phase,
> You want to be clear,
> you don't want
> to be muddled,
> What state are you in
> when you're
> feeling befuddled?

Riddle 18

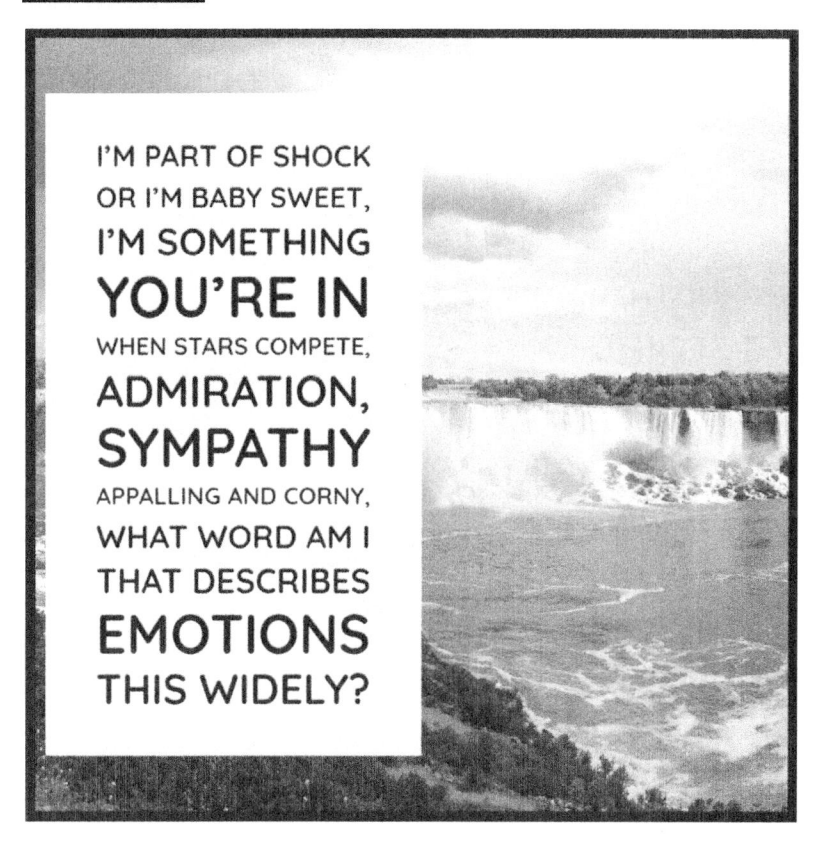

I'M PART OF SHOCK OR I'M BABY SWEET, I'M SOMETHING **YOU'RE IN** WHEN STARS COMPETE, **ADMIRATION, SYMPATHY** APPALLING AND CORNY, WHAT WORD AM I THAT DESCRIBES **EMOTIONS** THIS WIDELY?

Riddle 19

YOU'RE EAGER **TO KNOW** OR YOU HAVE CONCERN, PUT ANOTHER WAY, IT'S SOMETHING **YOU EARN, AND WHEN** YOU HAVE THIS YOU'RE WILLING **TO LEARN,** WHAT AM I?

Riddle 20

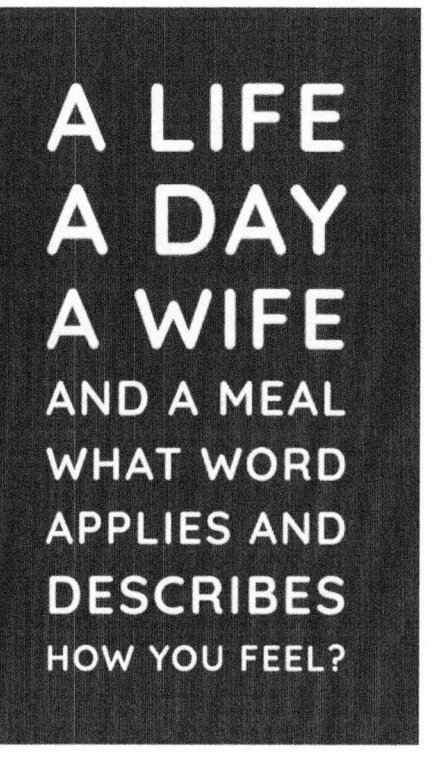

A LIFE
A DAY
A WIFE
AND A MEAL
WHAT WORD
APPLIES AND
DESCRIBES
HOW YOU FEEL?

Chapter Three
Homonyms

"These riddle answers feature words that have the same spelling, the same pronunciation but have different meanings"

Homonyms

Riddle 21

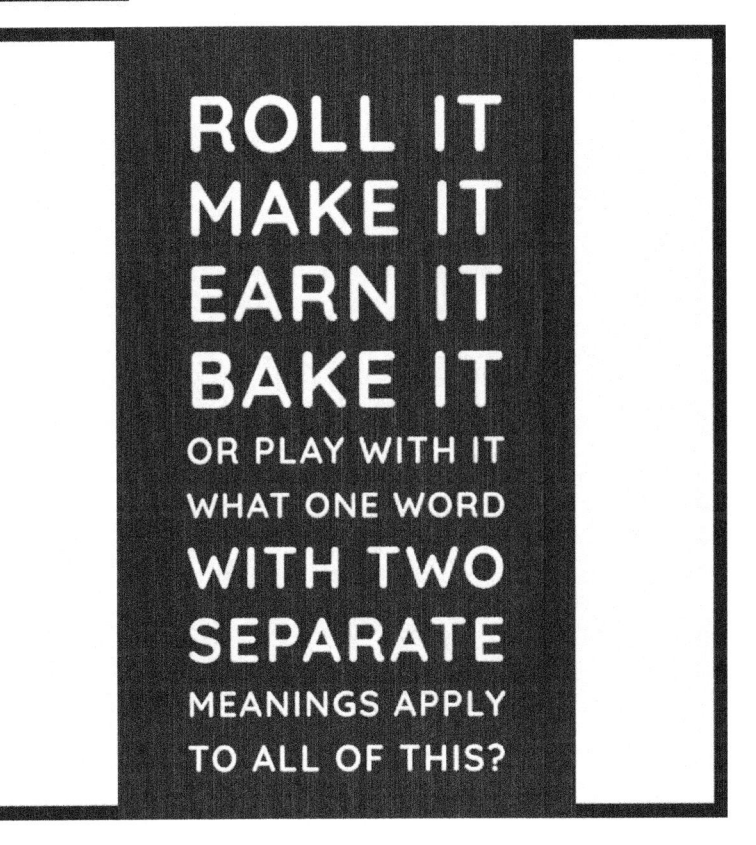

ROLL IT
MAKE IT
EARN IT
BAKE IT
OR PLAY WITH IT
WHAT ONE WORD
WITH TWO
SEPARATE
MEANINGS APPLY
TO ALL OF THIS?

Riddle 22

I am what precedes
the joining of two,
I'm when you're committed
to what you have to do,
with me you're attentive,
and involved, and I can
cause celebration,
what double meaning word
represents interest
and dedication?

Riddle 23

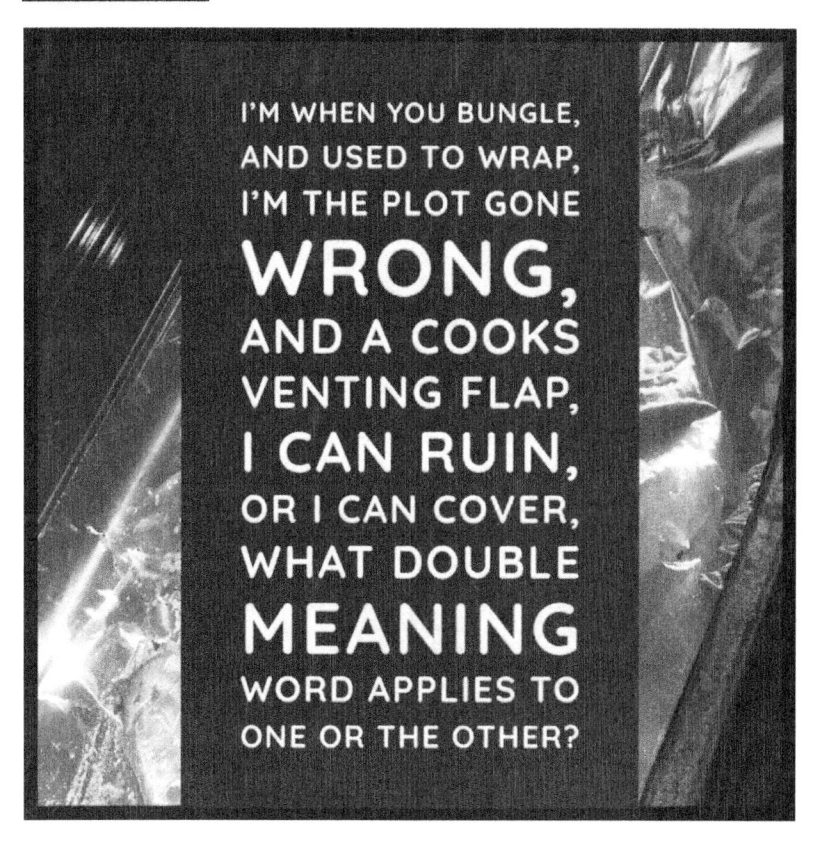

I'M WHEN YOU BUNGLE, AND USED TO WRAP, I'M THE PLOT GONE **WRONG**, AND A COOKS VENTING FLAP, I CAN RUIN, OR I CAN COVER, WHAT DOUBLE **MEANING** WORD APPLIES TO ONE OR THE OTHER?

Riddle 24

PRACTICE
THOMAS
RAILS
DRAGONS
TICKETS
AND A COACH
ALL RELATE TO ME,
WHAT WORD AM I
THAT GOES UNDERGROUND
AND IS A PART OF A TEAM?

Riddle 25

I am a word
that lives in the now,
and is the movement
of a stream,
I'm referenced in both
meteorology and rivers,
and apply whether
mild or extreme,
What double meaning
word am I?

Riddle 26

I'm a layout
and a plan,
and what's
generated by
a fan,
sketch me
and you'll get me,
or I can make
you chilly,
What word am I?

Riddle 27

I CAN IMPROVE MEALS AND THERE'S FOUR OF ME, **I ADD SPICE** TO LIFE, LITERALLY, I REPRESENT CHANGE AND **THAT CHANGE MAY URGE YOU TO REDECORATE AND REARRANGE,** WHAT DOUBLE MEANING WORD **HAS THIS** BROAD OF A RANGE?

Riddle 28

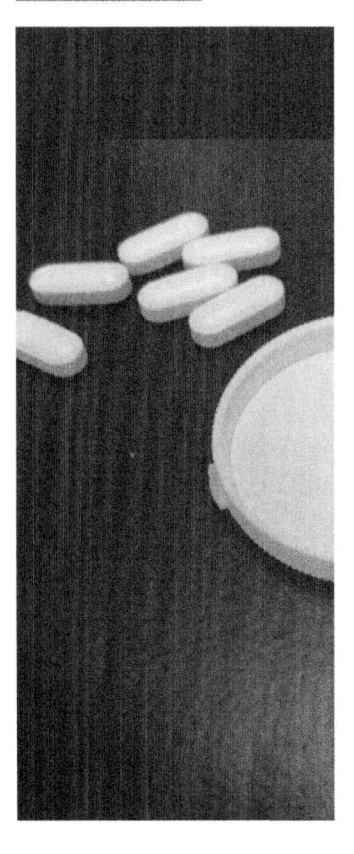

I HAVE TO BE LICENSED, **I ALSO FALSIFY,** I MIGHT NEEDLE YOU NOW AND THEN AND **MAKE YOU CRY, I SOMETIMES HAVE MY SAY ABOUT YOUR** DIRECTION OR FATE, **WHAT DOUBLE MEANING WORD** MEANS TO HELP OR **MANIPULATE?**

Riddle 29

I am a title
and I instruct,
I'm also another
name for a bus,
I'm a level of travel,
and I explain,
What word am I
that also relates
to a train?

Riddle 30

I'm quite heated,
so stay away,
I'm also what happens
when you lose your pay,
Sometimes I'm relaxing
to stare at all day,
but only when controlled,
and when there's
no foul play,
What word am I?

Chapter Four are Homograph Words

"These riddle answers feature words that are spelled the same but sound different and have different meanings"

Homographs

Riddle 31

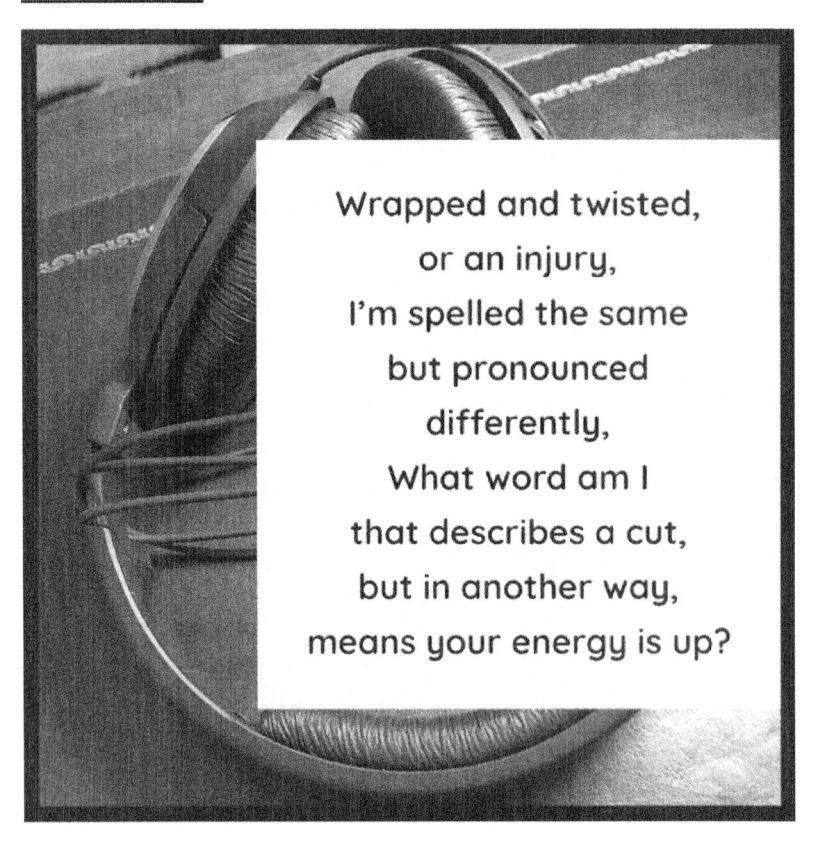

Wrapped and twisted,
or an injury,
I'm spelled the same
but pronounced
differently,
What word am I
that describes a cut,
but in another way,
means your energy is up?

Riddle 32

I ruin hair
and can start a toy,
I can't be seen,
but I can destroy,
pronounced two ways,
I mean different things,
What word am I
that helps support
wings?

Riddle 33

I'm really smelly,
said differently
I'm a skill,
stinky me is
full of waste,
talented me
can cinch a waist,
What one word
covers these two:
A specific talent
that relates to poo?

Riddle 34

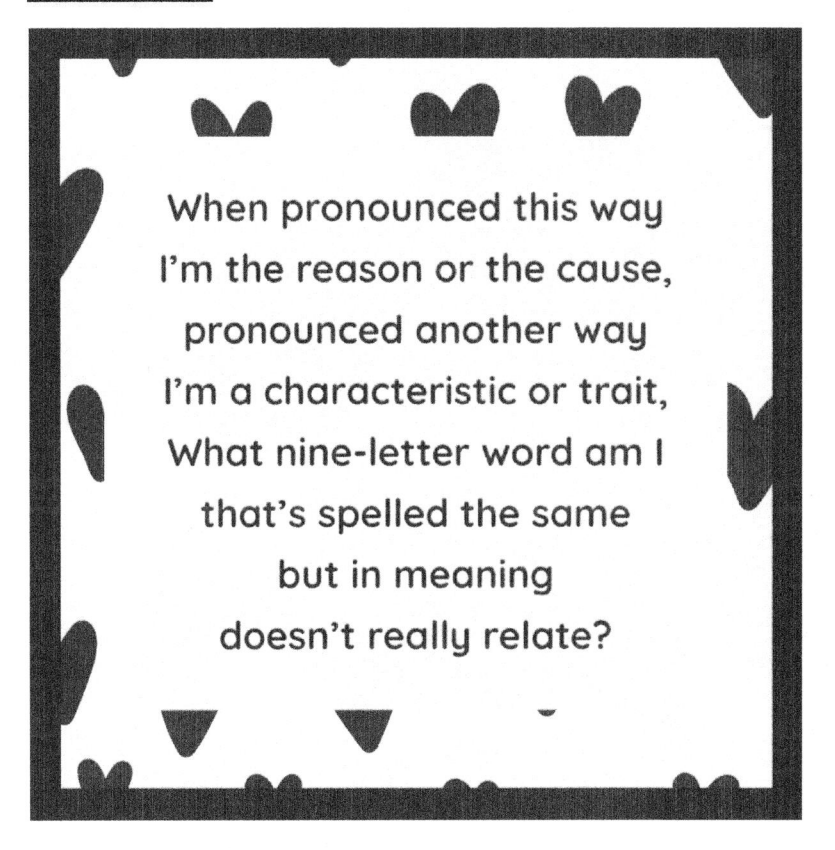

When pronounced this way
I'm the reason or the cause,
pronounced another way
I'm a characteristic or trait,
What nine-letter word am I
that's spelled the same
but in meaning
doesn't really relate?

Riddle 35

Consecrated, sacred, and holy,
is the God to whom some pray,
For others I'm merely good fortune
when pronounced another way,
spelled the same,
said with one syllable or two,
What word am I that's both
divine, and the lucky few?

Riddle 36

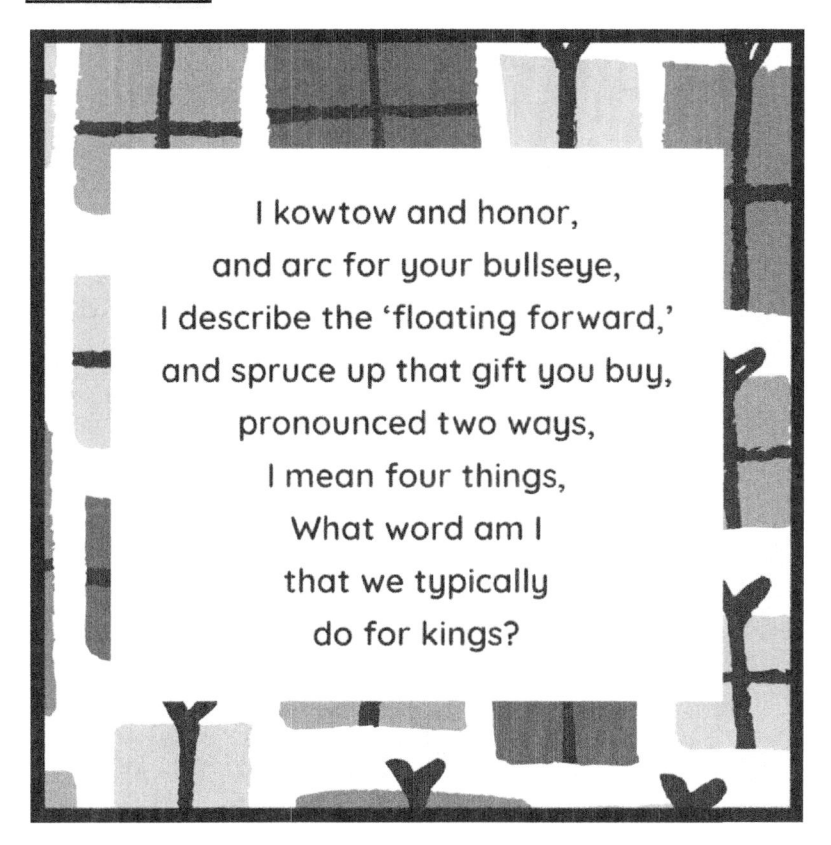

I kowtow and honor,
and arc for your bullseye,
I describe the 'floating forward,'
and spruce up that gift you buy,
pronounced two ways,
I mean four things,
What word am I
that we typically
do for kings?

Riddle 37

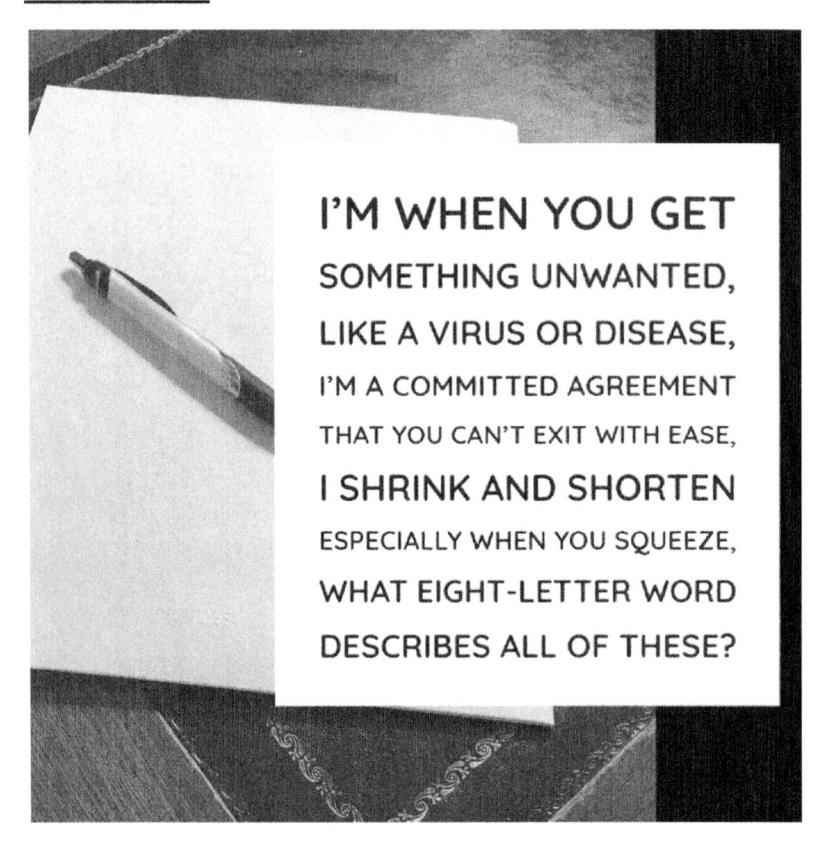

I'M WHEN YOU GET SOMETHING UNWANTED, LIKE A VIRUS OR DISEASE, I'M A COMMITTED AGREEMENT THAT YOU CAN'T EXIT WITH EASE, I SHRINK AND SHORTEN ESPECIALLY WHEN YOU SQUEEZE, WHAT EIGHT-LETTER WORD DESCRIBES ALL OF THESE?

Riddle 38

Abandon,
quit,
leave,
or arid,
hot,
and dry,
are multiple meanings
for this six-letter word,
Can you guess it?
What word am I?

Riddle 39

To some,
I'm insignificant,
Give one,
wait for one,
or get one,
Pronounced two ways
directly or indirectly
I apply to time,
What itty-bitty word
do these clues define?

Riddle 40

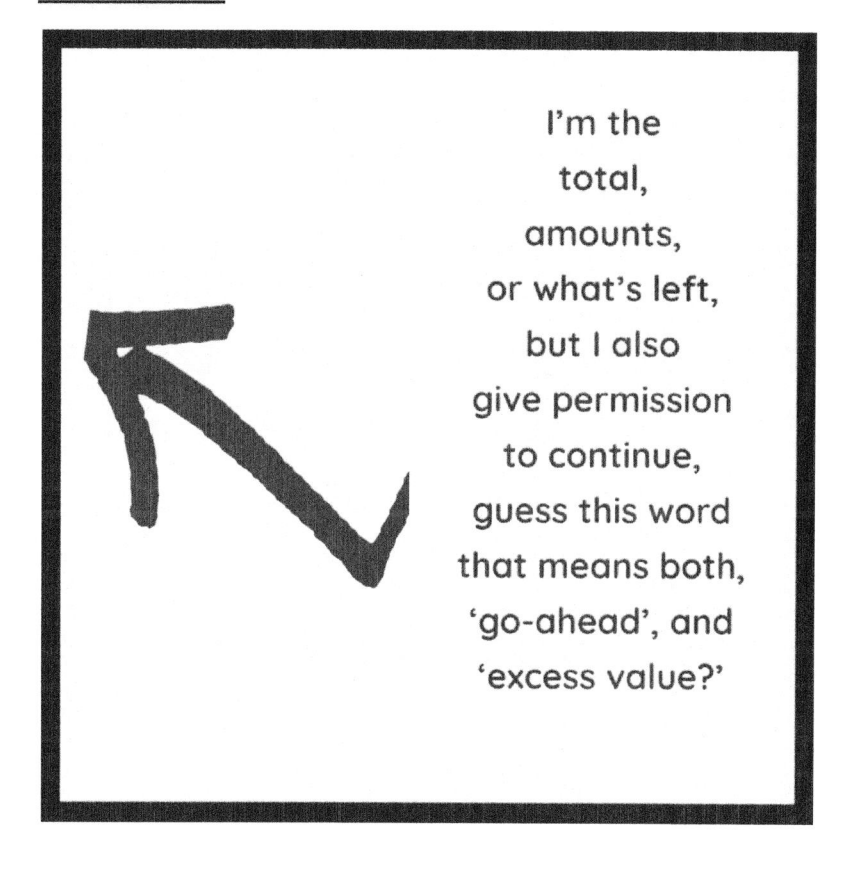

I'm the
total,
amounts,
or what's left,
but I also
give permission
to continue,
guess this word
that means both,
'go-ahead', and
'excess value?'

Chapter Five Triple Homophones

"These riddle answers feature three words with the same pronunciation but have different meanings and also different spelling"

Triple Homophones

Riddle 41

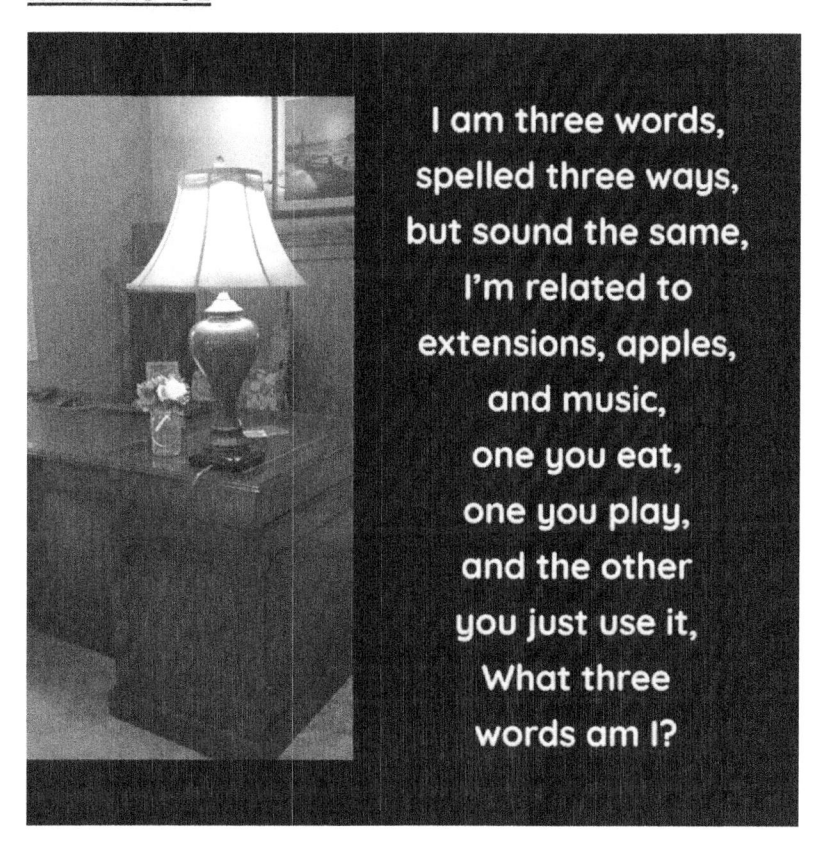

I am three words,
spelled three ways,
but sound the same,
I'm related to
extensions, apples,
and music,
one you eat,
one you play,
and the other
you just use it,
What three
words am I?

Riddle 42

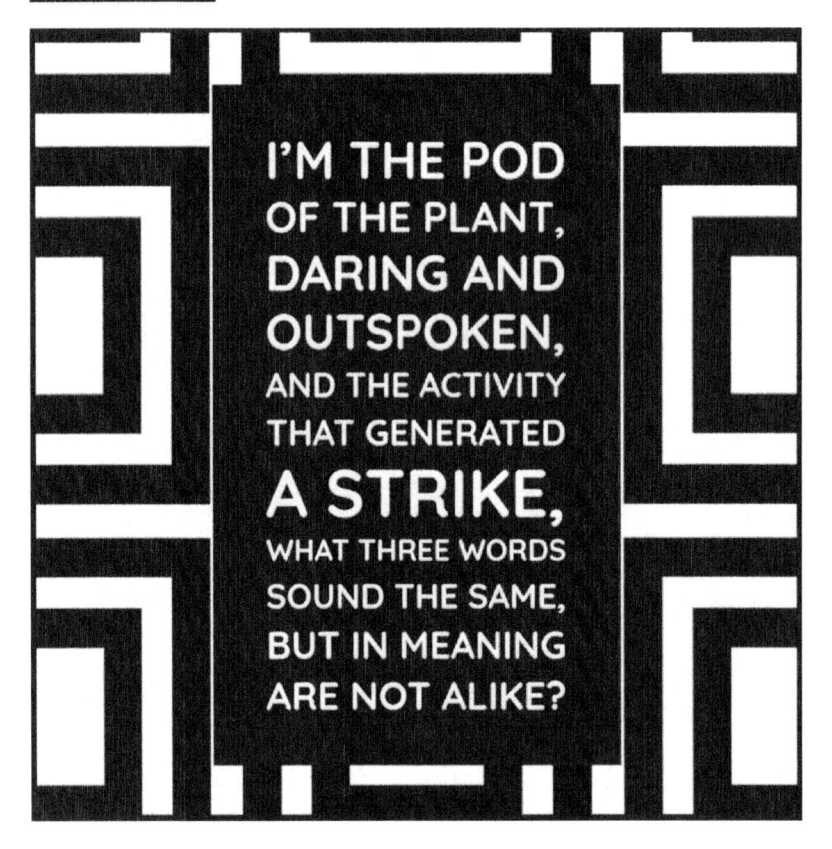

I'M THE POD OF THE PLANT, DARING AND OUTSPOKEN, AND THE ACTIVITY THAT GENERATED A STRIKE, WHAT THREE WORDS SOUND THE SAME, BUT IN MEANING ARE NOT ALIKE?

Riddle 43

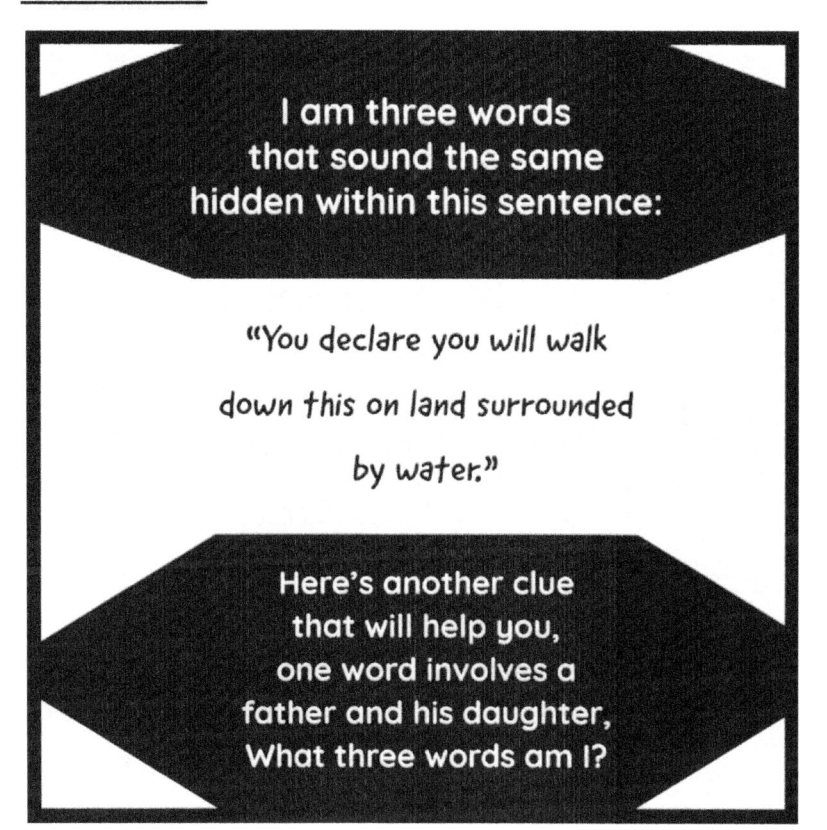

I am three words that sound the same hidden within this sentence:

"You declare you will walk down this on land surrounded by water."

Here's another clue that will help you, one word involves a father and his daughter, What three words am I?

Riddle 44

"I barfed when I flapped above the chimney."

What three words that sound the same, directly or indirectly, apply to the above sentence?
Solve it quickly!

Riddle 45

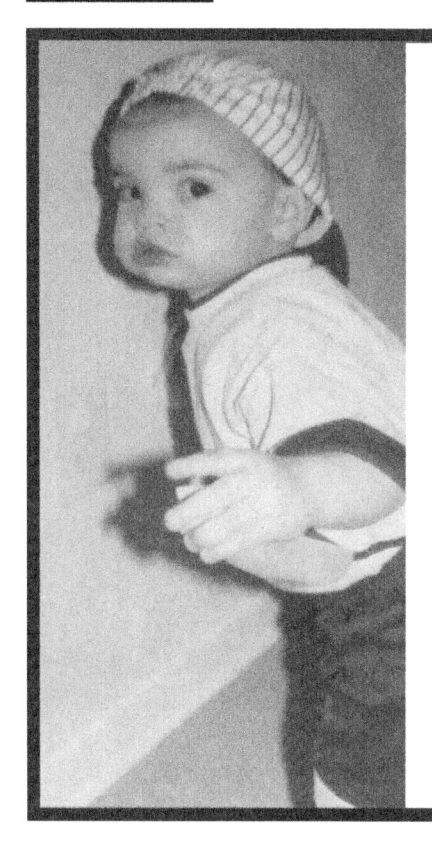

YOU GAINED KNOWLEDGE; IT MEANS YOU WERE THIS, SNUG, STIFF, TENSE, OR GIVE IT A TWIST, YOUNG AND SMALL DESCRIBES THE LITTLE FELLA OR LITTLE MISS, WHAT THREE WORDS SOUND ALIKE, BUT MEAN DIFFERENT THINGS, GO AHEAD, TAKE A GUESS?

Riddle 46

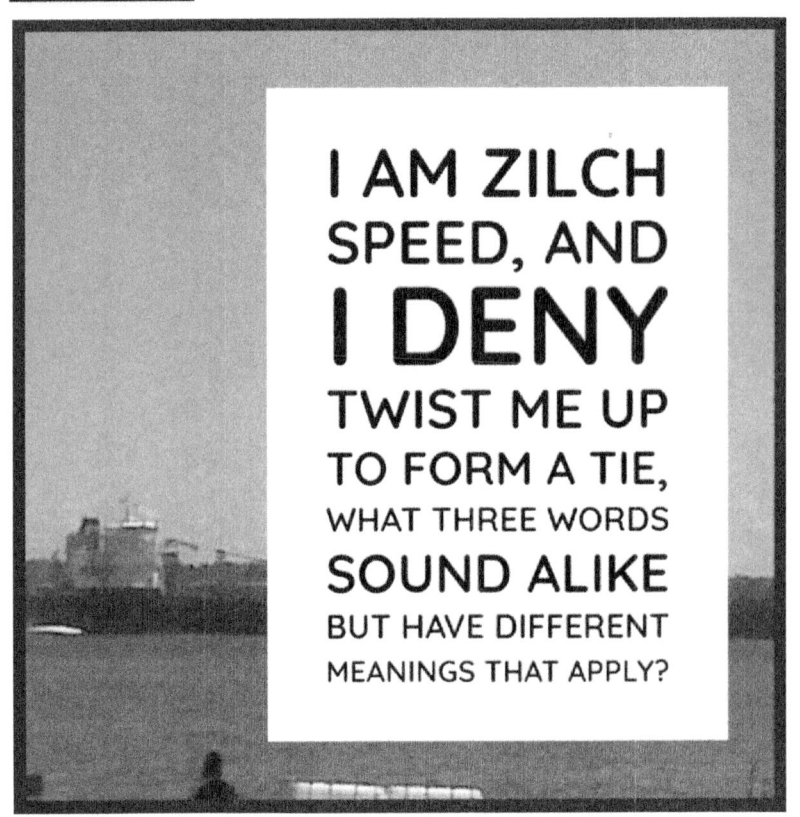

I AM ZILCH SPEED, AND I DENY TWIST ME UP TO FORM A TIE, WHAT THREE WORDS SOUND ALIKE BUT HAVE DIFFERENT MEANINGS THAT APPLY?

Riddle 47

REMOVE AN OUTER COATING, SPELLED DIFFERENTLY, I GROW ON A TREE, I'M JUST A COUPLE DEFINITELY NOT THREE, WHAT WORDS ARE THESE, WHAT CAN THEY BE?

Riddle 48

Go this direction,
use a scale,
or put me in a drink
to make protein ale,
These three words
sound alike;
Referring to vicinity,
supplements and
the action involved
with a measuring device,
What words are they?

Riddle 49

"He sniveled with discontent, twisted the crank, then it went, celebrating success, he then did this and dined."

What three words that sound the same fit his story? What comes to mind?

Riddle 50

I'm just one,
or mailed and gone,
I'm what you smell
when you put me on,
What three words
describe all of these,
and sound the same but
are spelled differently?

Chapter Six Double Homophones

"These riddle answers feature two words that sound alike but have different meanings and different spelling"

Double Homophones

Riddle 51

I am two words;
Rub me on,
or I can rub you out,
"lotion-explosion"
describes them both,
but if you're
a part of the latter
you could end up
under oath!
What two words am I?

Riddle 52

> Spelled two ways,
> I sound the same;
> One way I'm naked,
> simple, and plain,
> My other meaning
> has to do with wild game,
> holding up, pushing down,
> and none of these meanings
> are the same. What word am I?

Riddle 53

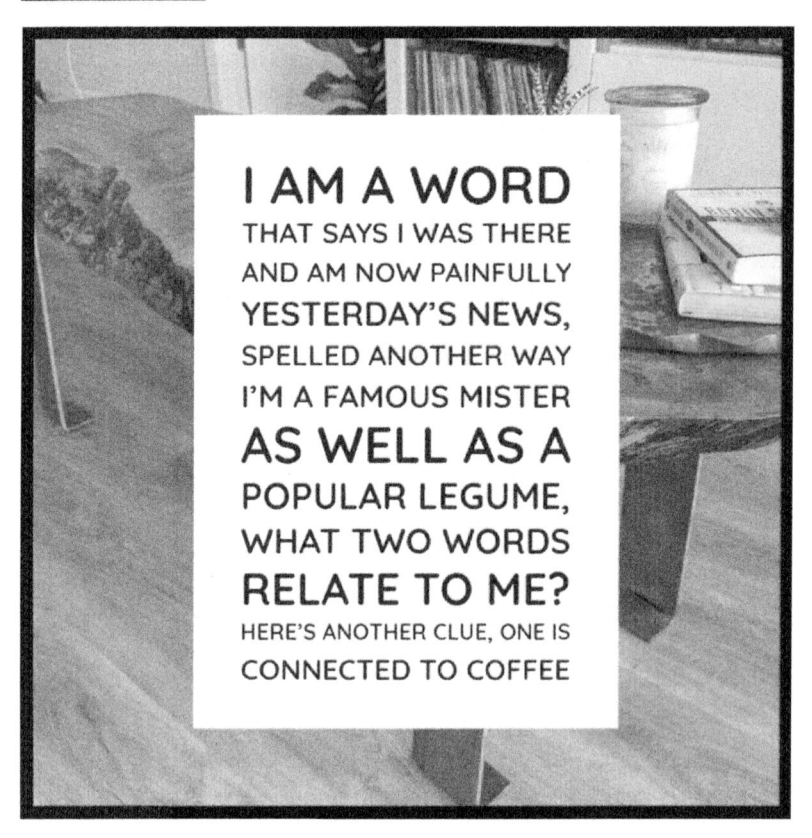

I AM A WORD THAT SAYS I WAS THERE AND AM NOW PAINFULLY YESTERDAY'S NEWS, SPELLED ANOTHER WAY I'M A FAMOUS MISTER AS WELL AS A POPULAR LEGUME, WHAT TWO WORDS RELATE TO ME? HERE'S ANOTHER CLUE, ONE IS CONNECTED TO COFFEE

Riddle 54

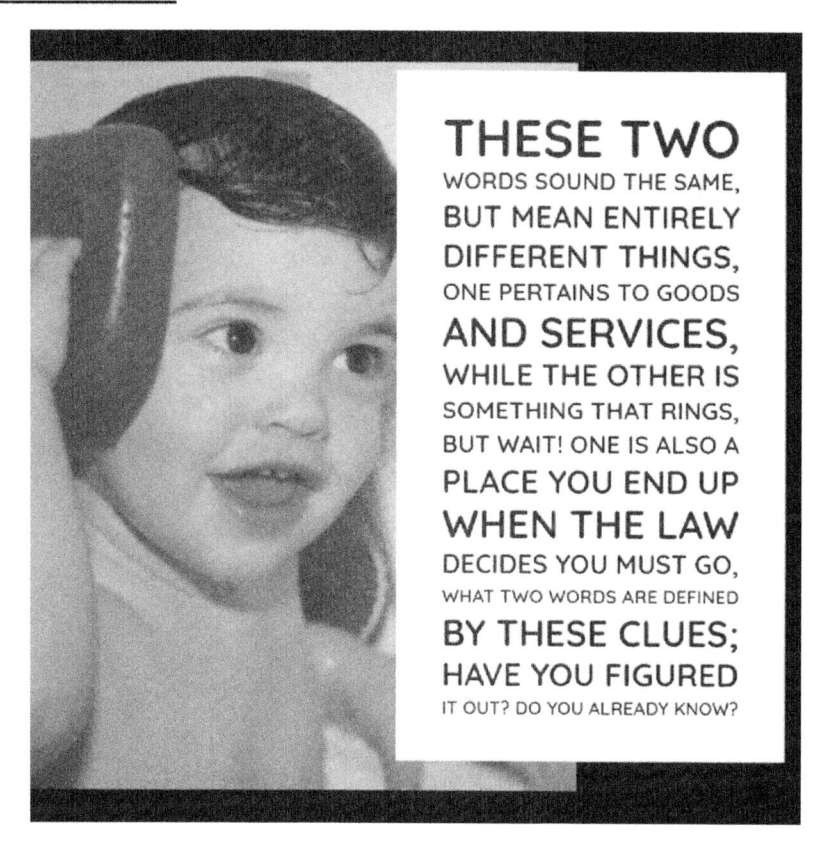

THESE TWO WORDS SOUND THE SAME, **BUT MEAN ENTIRELY DIFFERENT THINGS,** ONE PERTAINS TO GOODS **AND SERVICES,** WHILE THE OTHER IS SOMETHING THAT RINGS, BUT WAIT! ONE IS ALSO A **PLACE YOU END UP WHEN THE LAW** DECIDES YOU MUST GO, WHAT TWO WORDS ARE DEFINED **BY THESE CLUES; HAVE YOU FIGURED** IT OUT? DO YOU ALREADY KNOW?

Riddle 55

I'M AN ANNUAL,
AND USED TO BAKE,
I CAN BE REAL,
OR I CAN BE FAKE,
I'M SOMETHING YOU PLANT,
OR IN SOMETHING
YOU MAKE,
WHAT TWO WORDS
SOUND THE SAME?
BUT ONE IS PRETTY,
WHILE THE
OTHER A GRAIN?

Riddle 56

I cause delays,
I make you wait,
I'm something you take
when you need a break,
Sounding the same
but spelled differently,
I also relate to four cute feet,
What two words apply to these;
One can smell like popcorn and cheese,
the other is something you take
when ill at ease?

Riddle 57

When I'm vanilla
I'm this,
When I'm basic
I'm this,
When I fly
I'm this,
When I'm level
I'm this,
I am two words
that sound the same
whose meanings
certainly are not,
Can you guess them?
Go ahead, give it a shot!

Riddle 58

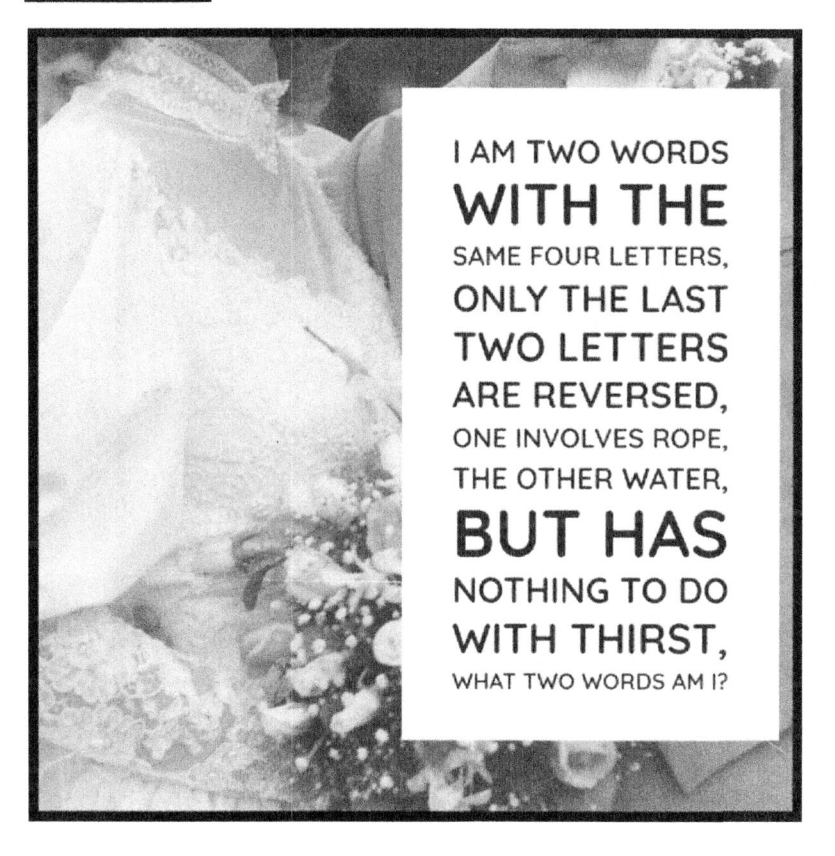

I AM TWO WORDS **WITH THE** SAME FOUR LETTERS, ONLY THE LAST TWO LETTERS ARE REVERSED, ONE INVOLVES ROPE, THE OTHER WATER, **BUT HAS** NOTHING TO DO WITH THIRST, WHAT TWO WORDS AM I?

Riddle 59

I am two words that
sound the same,
but in no way are alike,
In one way you disagree,
go toe-to-toe and
put up a valiant fight,
The other pertains to
the clothes you had on
when you went out
the other night,
What two words am I?

Riddle 60

These two words
can be indirectly related,
and they sound the same,
You triumphed and conquered
and took first place,
and the trophy will
feature your name,
Guess these two three-letter words,
In both cases they can
lead to fame!

Chapter Seven Words With "Q" in Them

"These riddle answers have the letter Q somewhere in the word itself, or begin with the letter Q"

Words With "Q" In them

Riddle 61

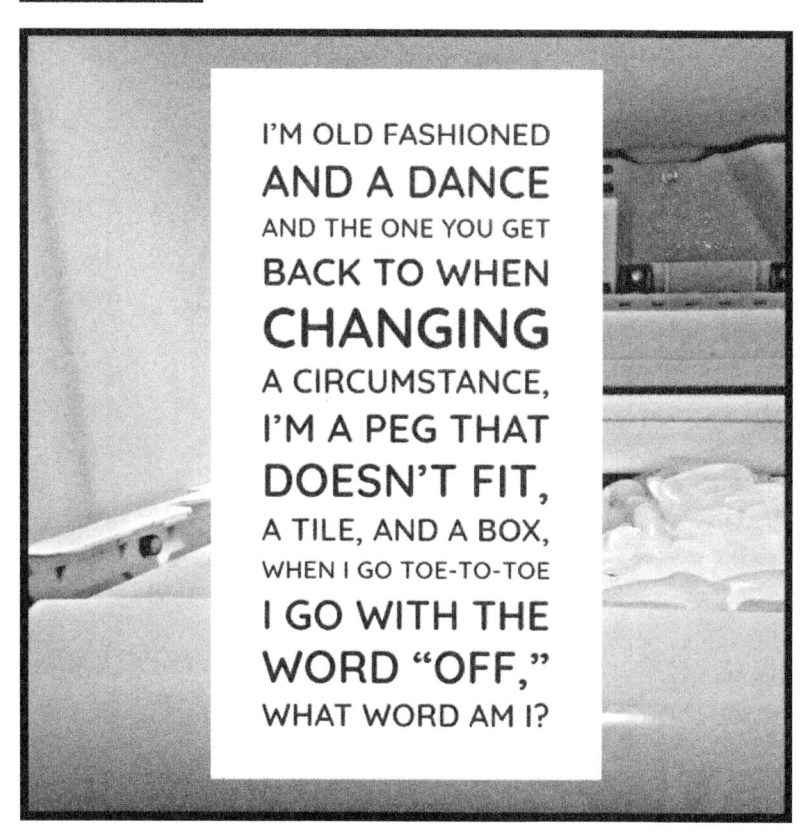

I'M OLD FASHIONED **AND A DANCE** AND THE ONE YOU GET **BACK TO WHEN CHANGING** A CIRCUMSTANCE, I'M A PEG THAT **DOESN'T FIT,** A TILE, AND A BOX, WHEN I GO TOE-TO-TOE **I GO WITH THE WORD "OFF,"** WHAT WORD AM I?

Riddle 62

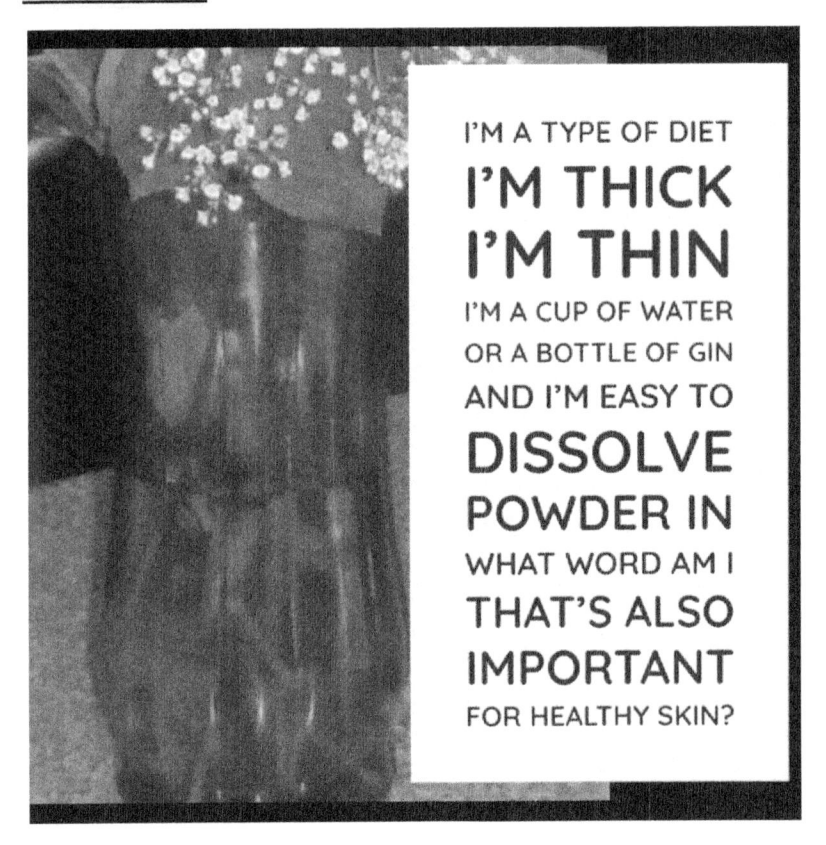

I'M A TYPE OF DIET
**I'M THICK
I'M THIN**
I'M A CUP OF WATER
OR A BOTTLE OF GIN
AND I'M EASY TO
**DISSOLVE
POWDER IN**
WHAT WORD AM I
**THAT'S ALSO
IMPORTANT**
FOR HEALTHY SKIN?

Riddle 63

Partners, portions
and treatment all
work best with this,
Branches of government
and sugar also apply
and I'm the better way
to cut a pie,
What word am I?

Riddle 64

I am something you make,
ask or inquire,
You might even beg
when the situation is dire,
When you solicit info for
whatever you're doing,
You're seeking answers
for what you're pursuing,
What word am I?

Riddle 65

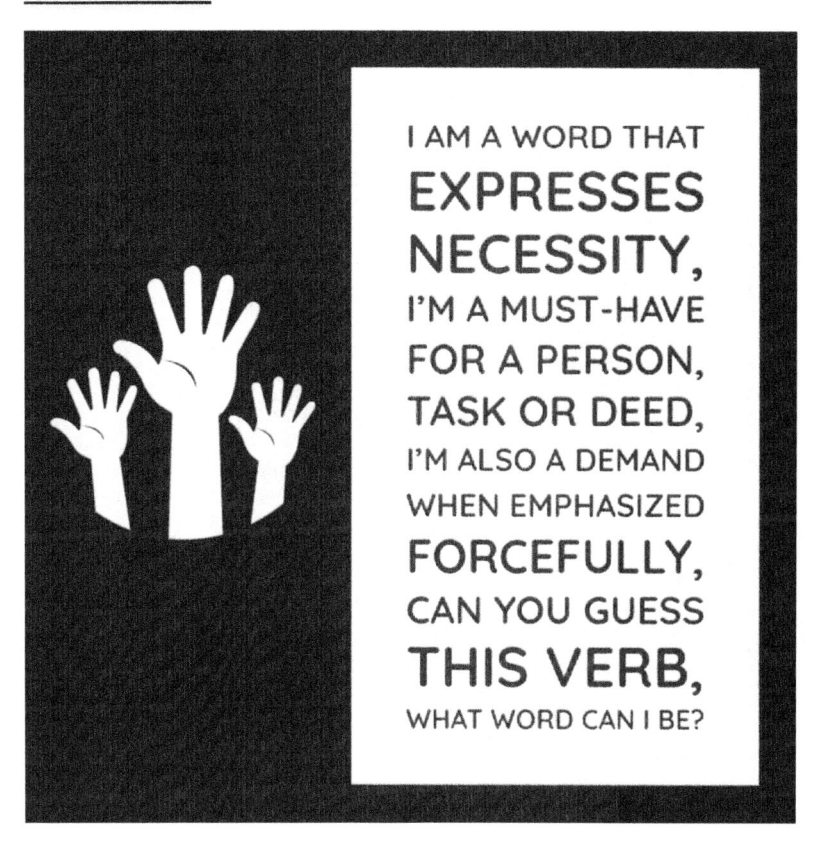

I AM A WORD THAT **EXPRESSES NECESSITY,** I'M A MUST-HAVE FOR A PERSON, TASK OR DEED, I'M ALSO A DEMAND WHEN EMPHASIZED **FORCEFULLY,** CAN YOU GUESS **THIS VERB,** WHAT WORD CAN I BE?

Riddle 66

I AM THE ARCHER'S CASE, AND IN ANOTHER WAY I TREMBLE AND SHAKE, **WHETHER** SCARED OR COLD, **I'M WHEN** YOU VIBRATE, WHAT WORD AM I **THAT FITS** THESE TRAITS?

Riddle 67

A knightly pursuit
is what I'm about
Finding the holy grail
is what it's all about,
This kind of mission
is a medieval expedition,
What word am I?
What's your intuition?

Riddle 68

I'm nontranslucent,
no light passes through,
by definition I could
be murky, or hindered by hue,
I'm also a way to cover
blemishes in photography,
This riddle isn't easy,
What word can I be?

Riddle 69

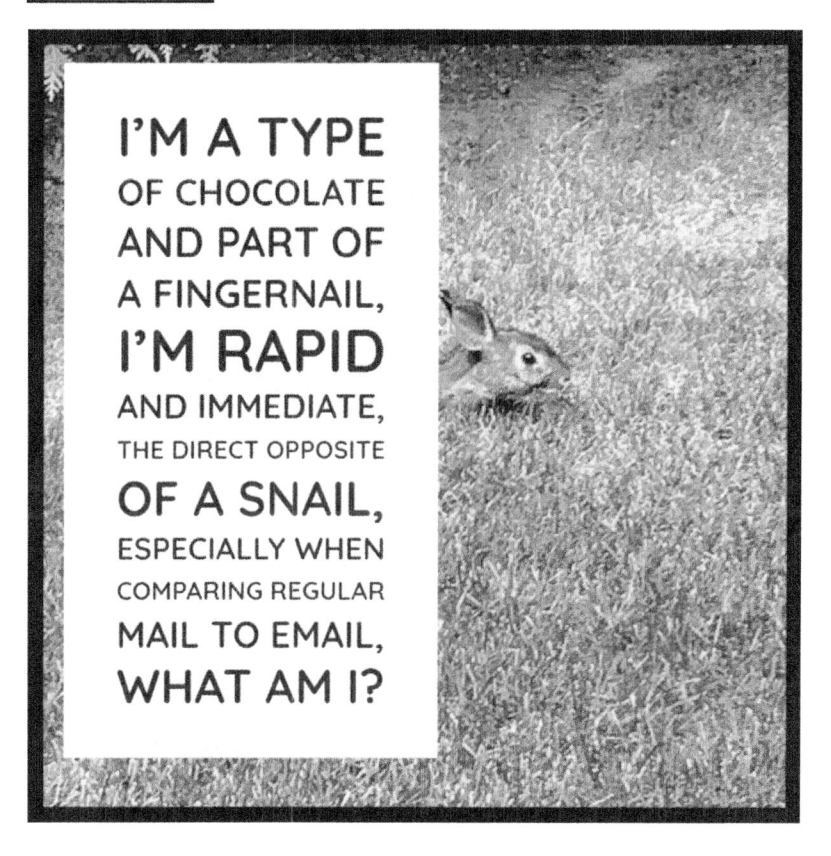

I'M A TYPE OF CHOCOLATE AND PART OF A FINGERNAIL, I'M RAPID AND IMMEDIATE, THE DIRECT OPPOSITE OF A SNAIL, ESPECIALLY WHEN COMPARING REGULAR MAIL TO EMAIL, WHAT AM I?

Riddle 70

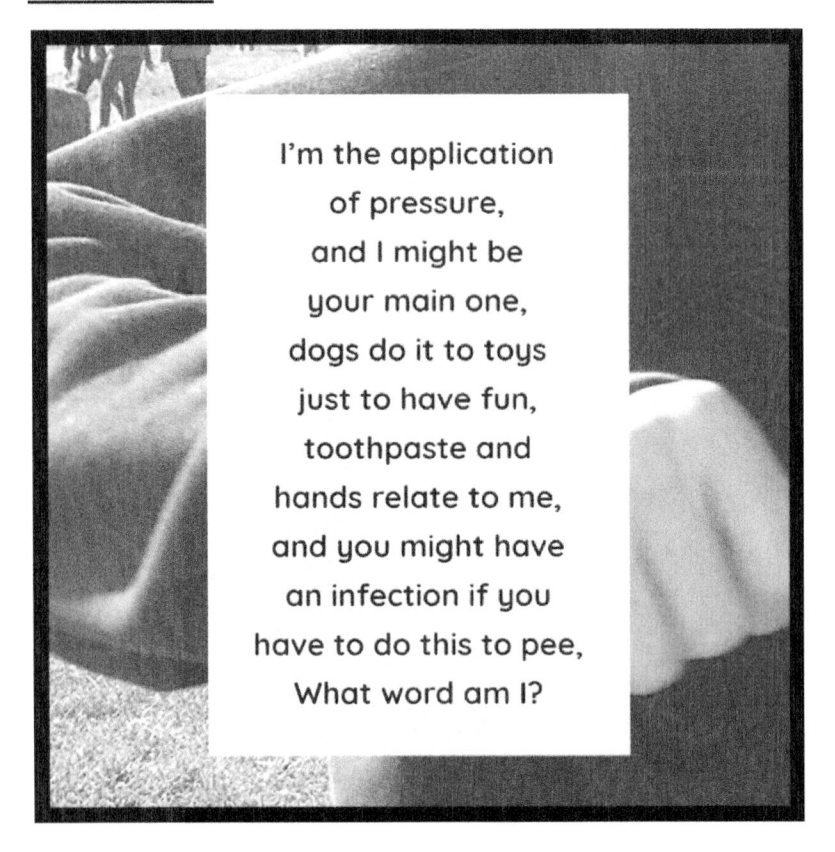

I'm the application
of pressure,
and I might be
your main one,
dogs do it to toys
just to have fun,
toothpaste and
hands relate to me,
and you might have
an infection if you
have to do this to pee,
What word am I?

Chapter Eight are Four Syllable Words

"These riddle answers feature words, from any topic, with four syllables"

Four Syllable Words

Riddle 71

Enjoy the movie,
celebrate the day,
I'm self-reliant,
and earn my own pay,
I claim self-rule
and I call myself free,
I'm sovereign,
reliable,
and exude autonomy,
What four-syllable
word am I?

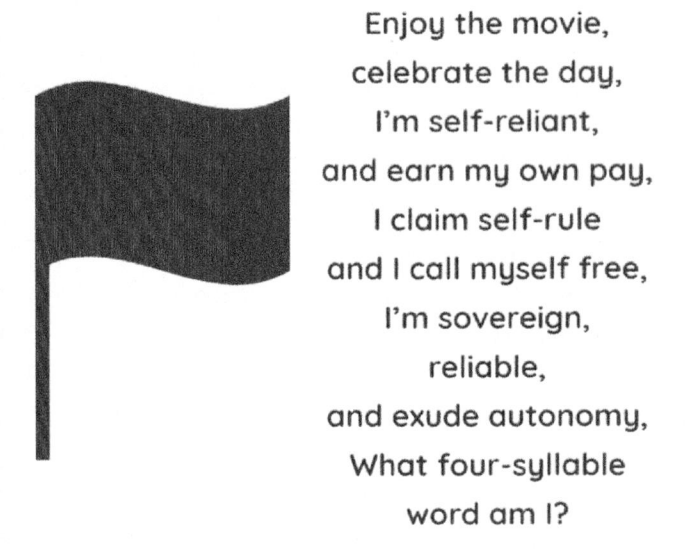

Riddle 72

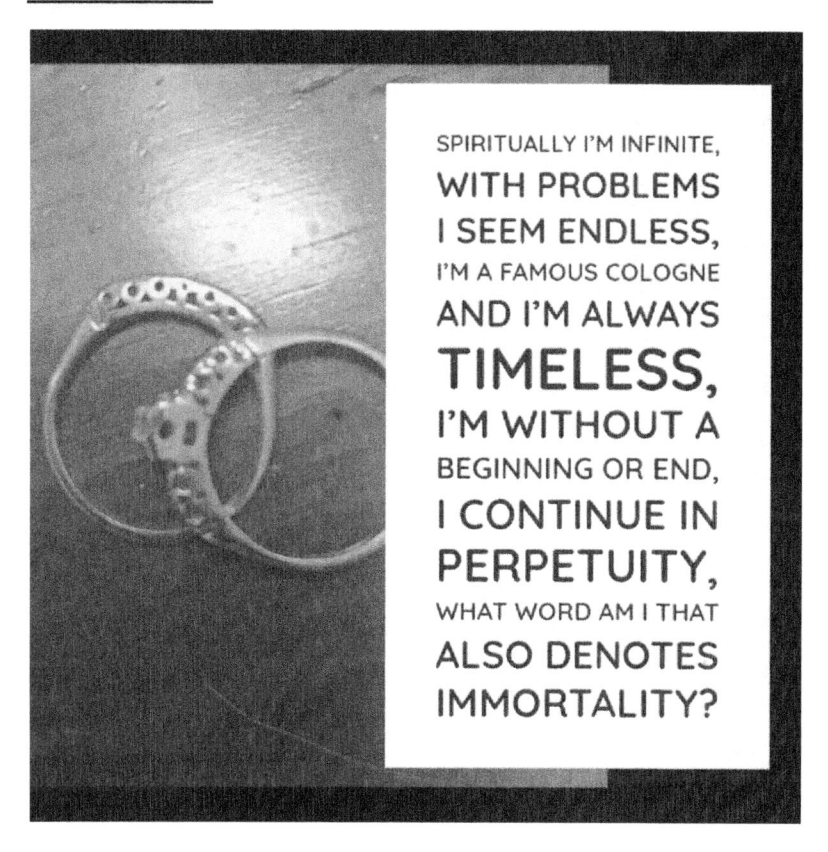

SPIRITUALLY I'M INFINITE, **WITH PROBLEMS I SEEM ENDLESS,** I'M A FAMOUS COLOGNE **AND I'M ALWAYS TIMELESS,** I'M WITHOUT A BEGINNING OR END, **I CONTINUE IN PERPETUITY,** WHAT WORD AM I THAT **ALSO DENOTES IMMORTALITY?**

Riddle 73

Some people are
this kind of junkie,
others can't absorb this,
It's needed to make
wiser decisions,
assuming sources
are reliable and legit,
What four-syllable
word is it?

Riddle 74

I am a four-syllable word
that's considered the flipside,
I apply to music,
facts and choices,
I'm your substitute course,
as well as a different
plan of action,
What word am I?

Riddle 75

I'm a plane,
ghost,
man,
bacteria
and ink,
What four-syllable word
applies to these,
take a guess,
What do you think?

Riddle 76

I apply to songs, plans, language, works and meanings, This four-syllable word is expressly unique and takes you back to the beginning, What word am I?

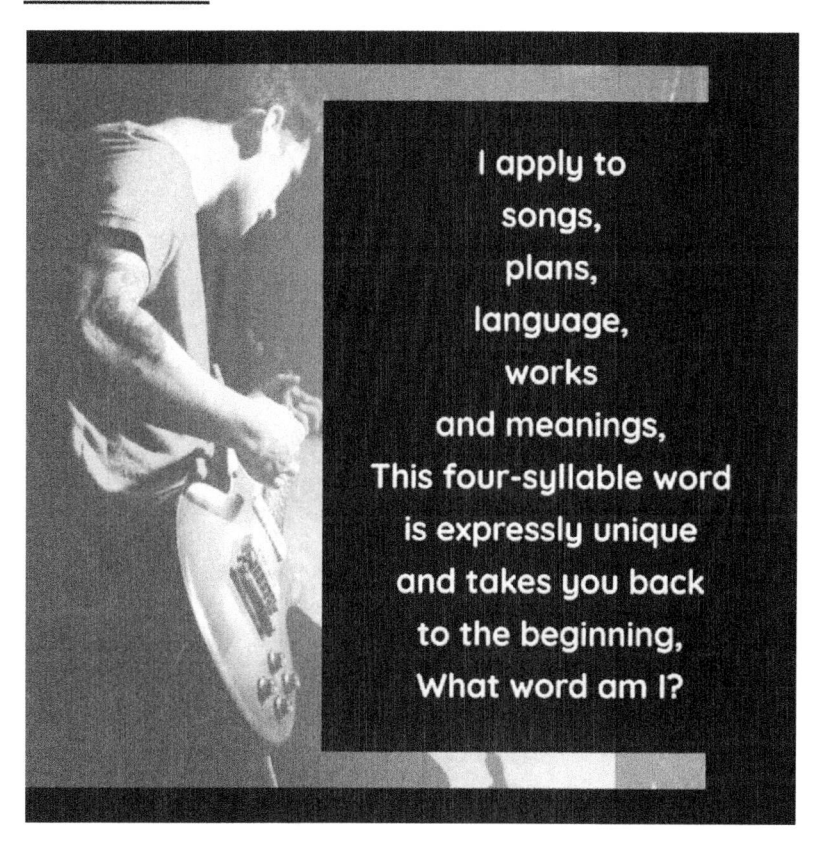

Riddle 77

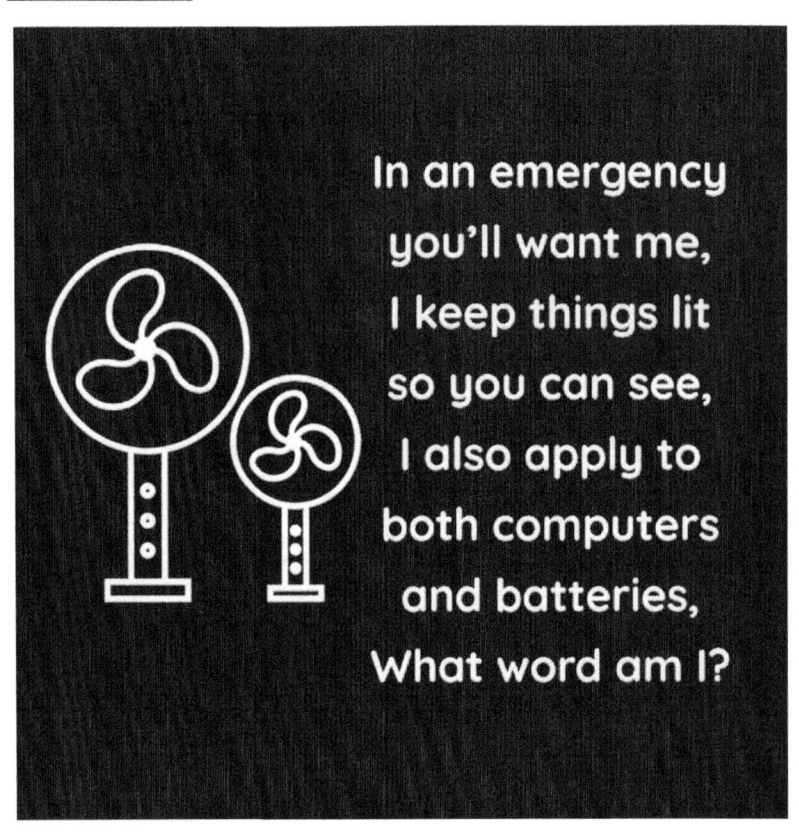

In an emergency you'll want me, I keep things lit so you can see, I also apply to both computers and batteries, What word am I?

Riddle 78

We reached a settlement,
We made the decision,
We had determination
and we set our intention,
Essentially we persevered,
What word am I
that even applies
to the New Year?

Riddle 79

> Make an attempt,
> give it a try,
> research before
> committing,
> like the science guy,
> trial and error,
> probe and study,
> just like that famous
> Professor that's Nutty,
> What word am I?

Riddle 80

I apply to a car, blinds, a washer and a reply
What four-syllable mechanized word am I?

Answer Section

Chapter One Answers

1. Brilliant

2. Confident

3. Generous

4. Insanity/Insane

5. Intelligence

6. Weak

7. Calm

8. Curious

9. Dedicated

10. Warmth

Chapter Two Answers

11. Powerful

12. Pride

13. Grief

14. Relaxed/Relax

15. Misery

16. Pain

17. Confused

18. Awe

19. Interest

20. Happy

Chapter Three Answers

21. Dough

22. Engaged

23. Foil

24. Train

25. Current

26. Draft

27. Season

28. Doctor

29. Coach

30. Fire

Chapter Four Answers

31. Wound

32. Wind

33. Sewer

34. Attribute

35. Blessed

36. Bow

37. Contract

38. Desert

39. Minute

40. Proceeds

Chapter Five Answers

41. Chord, Cord, Cored

42. Bold, Bolled, Bowled

43. Aisle, I'll, Isle

44. Flew, Flu, Flue

45. Taught, Taut, Tot

46. Knot, Naught, Not

47. Pair, Pare, Pear

48. Way, Weigh, Whey

49. Whined, Wind, Wined

50. Cent, Scent, Sent

Chapter Six Answers

51. Balm/Bomb

52. Bare/Bear

53. Bean/Been

54. Cell/Sell

55. Flour/Flower

56. Pause/Paws

57. Plain/Plane

58. Tide/Tied

59. War/Wore

60. Won/One

Chapter Seven Answers

61. Square

62. Liquid

63. Equal

64. Request

65. Require

66. Quiver

67. Quest

68. Opaque

69. Quick

70. Squeeze

Chapter Eight Answers

71. Independence

72. Eternity

73. Information

74. Alternative

75. Invisible

76. Original

77. Generator

78. Resolution

79. Experiment

80. Automatic

Back Cover Answer

Warn/Worn

About the Author

I'm a daughter, sister, wife, mother, step-mother, grandmother, aunt, cousin, and friend.

My professional background is in telecommunications, real estate, and I currently own and operate three websites, including StumpedRiddles.com.

I completed my first book in October 2019. It's a book of personal poems spanning fifty years, called *"We Will Have Morning Smiles."*

This riddle book is part of an ongoing series of riddle books.

Why a Riddle Book?

I've always had this crazy ability to write riddles, sayings, poems, greetings, and one-liners. It's genetic or something?

It seems my comedic, serious, poetic, one-liner skills extend to writing.

So, instead of just rambling riddles to challenge the family, I thought, what the heck, let's do a riddle book or two or more.

Additional Riddle Books

Keep challenging yourself online with riddles featured at StumpedRiddles.com. There you can Subscribe to receive new riddle challenges.

Look for the 'Subscribe' box at the bottom of each website page or in the sidebar of the website pages.

Find Riddle Books at:

StumpedRiddles.com/category/riddlebooks/

Instant Party Riddles - #Stumped Volume 1

School Riddles - #Stumped Volume 2

Birthday Riddles - #Stumped Volume 3

Boredom Buster Riddles - #Stumped Volume 4

Halloween Riddles - #Stumped Volume 5

Christmas Riddles - #Stumped Volume 7

Be sure to check back for all your wacky riddle needs.

Social Media Follows:

1. Instagram.com/riddlechallenge

2. Twitter.com/stumpedriddles

3. Stumpedriddles.com

4. Facebook.com/stumpedriddles

Write Your Own Riddle

Here's your riddle challenge. Try to write your own riddle. You'll start with the answer, then go from there.

The Answer Is:
"Curtains"

Write your completed riddle in the box! Good Luck!

Printed in Great Britain
by Amazon